Swing trading: Full mastery course from beginner to advance level

1. Introduction

- **Definition of swing trading**
- **Why swing trading is a popular trading strategy**
- **Brief overview of book**

2. Understanding the market

- Market Analysis
- Types of market trend
- Understanding market cycles

3. Identifying entry and exit points

- Key technical indicators
- Understanding support and Resistance levels
- Reading candlestick charts
- Setting stop losses

4. Building a swing trading plan

- Risk management
- Position sizing
- Setting goals and objectives
- Developing a trading plan

5. Implementing your swing trading plan

- Finding stocks to trade
- Executing trades
- Monitoring your trades
- Making Adjustments to your plan

6. Advances swing trading techniques

- Swing trading with options
- Swing trading with futures
- Swing trading with forex

7. Conclusion

- Final thoughts on Swing trading Mastery

Swing trading introduction

Swing trading
Introduction

Swing trading is a type of short-term trading strategy that is used to capture price changes (or "swings") in the financial markets, such as stocks, bonds, currencies, commodities, and other instruments. Swing traders hold their positions for several days to several weeks, seeking to profit from the price swings in the market. The goal is to identify trends and make trades that profit from those trends as they develop over time. Swing traders use a variety of technical analysis tools, such as trend lines, support and resistance levels, and chart patterns, to make informed trading decisions.

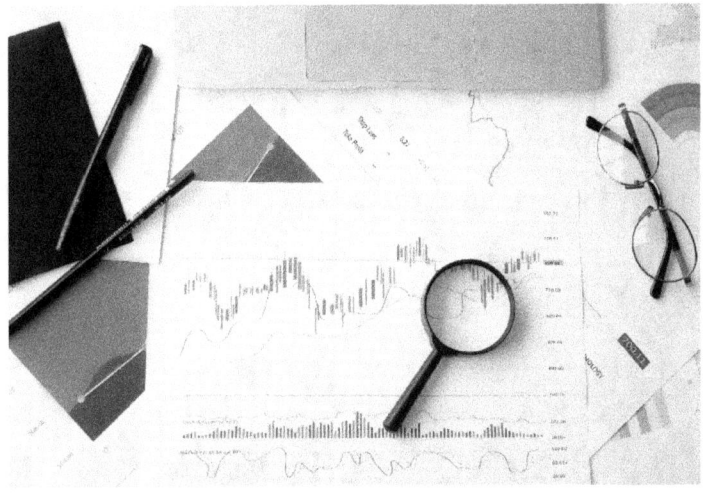

Definition of swing trading

Swing trading is a form of short to medium-term trading that aims to take advantage of price changes, or "swings," in the market. It involves holding a position for several days to several weeks in an attempt to profit from the price swings in the market. The objective of swing trading is to identify trends and make trades that benefit from those trends as they develop over time. This is accomplished by using technical analysis techniques, such as chart patterns, trend lines, and support and resistance levels, to make informed trading decisions. The goal of swing trading is to generate a profit by capturing a portion of the price swing in the market, rather than trying to hold a position for an extended period.

Why swing trading is a popular trading strategy

Swing trading is a popular trading strategy for several reasons:

1.   **Short-term focus:** Swing trading is a

short to medium-term trading strategy that allows traders to profit from price swings in the market, without having to hold a position for an extended period. This makes it an attractive option for those who do not want to hold a trade for an extended period.

2. **Flexibility:** Swing trading allows traders

to take advantage of both up and down trends in the market, providing a degree of flexibility that is not available with other trading strategies.

3.   **Reduced risk:** Because swing traders only hold their positions for several days to several weeks, they are exposed to less market risk compared to long-

term traders who hold positions for months or even years.

4. **Technical analysis** focus: Swing trading relies heavily on technical analysis techniques, such as chart patterns and trend lines, to make informed trading decisions. This makes it an attractive option for traders who prefer to use a systematic

and technical approach to trading.

5. **Suitable for all market conditions**: Swing trading can be applied to various financial instruments and markets, including stocks, bonds, commodities, currencies, and others, and is therefore suitable for all market conditions.

Overall, swing trading is a popular trading strategy because it offers traders a flexible and systematic approach to trading with a short-term focus, reduced risk, and the ability to profit from both up and down trends in the market.

Brief overview of Swing trading book

A swing trading book is typically a guide that provides an overview of the swing trading strategy and how to implement it in the financial markets. A good swing trading book should cover the following topics:

1. **Introduction to swing trading:** This section provides an overview of the swing trading strategy, including its history, goals, and objectives.

2. **Market analysis:** This section covers the basics of market analysis and how to use technical analysis techniques, such as trend lines, chart patterns, and support

and resistance levels, to identify trading opportunities.

3. **Trading psychology**: This section covers the importance of managing emotions, controlling risk, and maintaining discipline in trading.

4. **Trading strategies**: This section provides an overview of various

swing trading strategies, including entry and exit techniques, position sizing, and trade management.

5. **Risk management:** This section covers the importance of risk management and how to develop a risk management plan that suits your trading style and goals.

6.   **Real-world examples:** This section provides real-world examples and case studies of swing trading, showing how the concepts and techniques covered in the book can be applied in practice.

7.   **Conclusion:** This section summarizes the key takeaways from the book and provides final

thoughts on swing trading.

Overall, a swing trading book should provide a comprehensive guide to swing trading, covering the key concepts, techniques, and strategies involved, as well as real-world examples and practical tips for success.

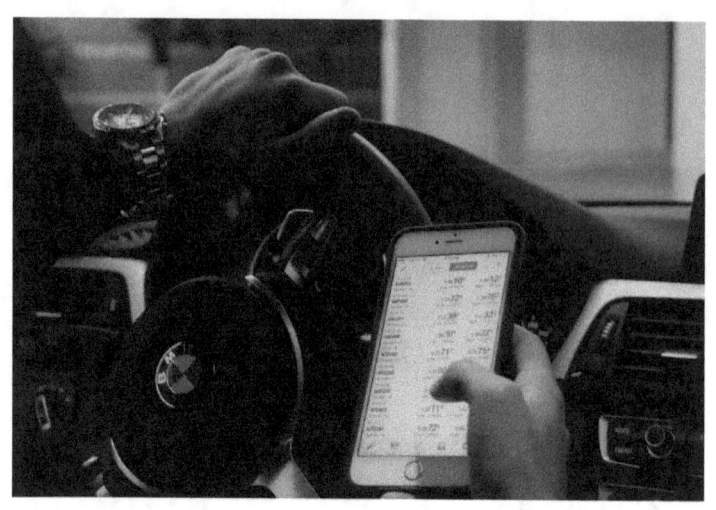

Understanding the market

Understanding the market is a crucial aspect of swing trading and other forms of trading. It involves analysing various market data and trends to identify opportunities to buy or sell a financial instrument and make a profit. Some of the key factors to consider when

understanding the market
include:

1. **Economic
   indicators**: This
   includes data such as
   gross domestic
   product (GDP),
   unemployment rate,
   inflation rate, and
   interest rate, which
   provide insights into
   the overall state of the
   economy and the
   direction of the
   market.

2.   **Market sentiment:** This refers to the overall mood or feeling of the market, which can be influenced by news events, rumours, and other factors.

3.   **Technical analysis:** This involves using charts and technical indicators, such as trend lines, moving averages, and

oscillators, to analyse price movements and identify trading opportunities.

4. **Company fundamentals**: This includes data such as revenue, earnings, and cash flow, which provide insights into the financial health of a company and can impact its stock price.

5. **Market news and events:** This includes

news and events related to the market and specific companies, such as earnings reports, mergers and acquisitions, and government policies, which can impact the market and provide trading opportunities.

By understanding the market, traders can make informed trading decisions and maximize

their chances of success.
However, it is important
to remember that the
market is inherently
uncertain and that past
performance is not a
guarantee of future
results.

Market analysis

Market analysis is a critical aspect of swing trading and other forms of trading that involves analysing various market data and trends to make informed trading decisions. The goal of market analysis is to identify patterns and opportunities in the market and make trades that bcnefit from those patterns. There are two main approaches to market analysis: fundamental analysis and technical analysis.

1. **Fundamental analysis:** This approach involves analysing economic, financial, and other qualitative and quantitative factors to assess the value of a security and make informed trading decisions. It looks at

factors such as a company's financial statements, management quality, and industry trends to determine its future prospects.

2. **Technical analysis:** This approach involves analysing price and volume data to identify patterns and make trading decisions. It uses

charts, technical indicators, and other tools to help traders make decisions based on past market performance. Technical analysis is based on the idea that market trends, as shown by charts and other technical indicators, tend to repeat themselves and can be used to predict future price movements.

Both fundamental analysis and technical analysis can be useful in market analysis, and many traders use a combination of both approaches to make informed trading decisions. However, it is important to remember that no analysis method is fool proof and that past performance is not a guarantee of future results. Market analysis is an ongoing process and traders must continuously monitor market trends and adjust their strategies as needed to stay ahead of the market.

Types of market trend

Market analysis is a critical aspect of swing trading and other forms of trading that involves analysing various market data and trends to make informed trading decisions. The goal of market analysis is to identify patterns and opportunities in the market and make trades that benefit from those patterns. There are two main approaches to market analysis: fundamental analysis and technical analysis.

1. **Fundamental analysis:** This approach involves analysing economic, financial, and other qualitative and quantitative factors to assess the value of a security and make

informed trading decisions. It looks at factors such as a company's financial statements, management quality, and industry trends to determine its future prospects.

2. **Technical analysis**: This approach involves analysing price and volume data to identify patterns and

make trading decisions. It uses charts, technical indicators, and other tools to help traders make decisions based on past market performance. Technical analysis is based on the idea that market trends, as shown by charts and other technical indicators, tend to repeat themselves and can be used to predict future price movements.

Both fundamental analysis and technical analysis can be useful in market analysis, and many traders use a combination of both approaches to make informed trading decisions. However, it is important to remember that no analysis method is fool proof and that past performance is not a guarantee of future results. Market analysis is an ongoing process and traders must continuously monitor market trends and adjust their strategies as needed to stay ahead of the market.

Understanding the market cycle

Market cycles refer to the recurring patterns of growth and decline that occur in financial markets over time. These cycles are driven by a variety of factors, including economic conditions, interest rates, and investor sentiment. There are several stages in a market cycle, including:

1.   **Expansion**: This is the stage of the market cycle in which the economy is growing, employment is rising, and consumer confidence is high. This is typically a bullish phase for the market, and prices for stocks and other financial

instruments tend to rise.

2. **Peak:** This is the stage in which the market has reached its highest point, and the economy is showing signs of slowing down. This is a time of uncertainty for investors, and prices may start to decline.

3. **Contraction:** This is the stage in which the economy is in

recession, employment is falling, and consumer confidence is low. This is typically a bearish phase for the market, and prices for stocks and other financial instruments tend to decline.

4.   **Trough:** This is the stage in which the market has reached its lowest point, and the economy is starting to

recover. This is a time of opportunity for investors, and prices may start to rise.

Market cycles are not always predictable, and the length and severity of each stage can vary greatly. However, by understanding the market cycles, traders can make informed trading decisions and position themselves to benefit from the ups and downs of the market. It is important to remember that the market is inherently uncertain and that past performance is not a guarantee of future results.

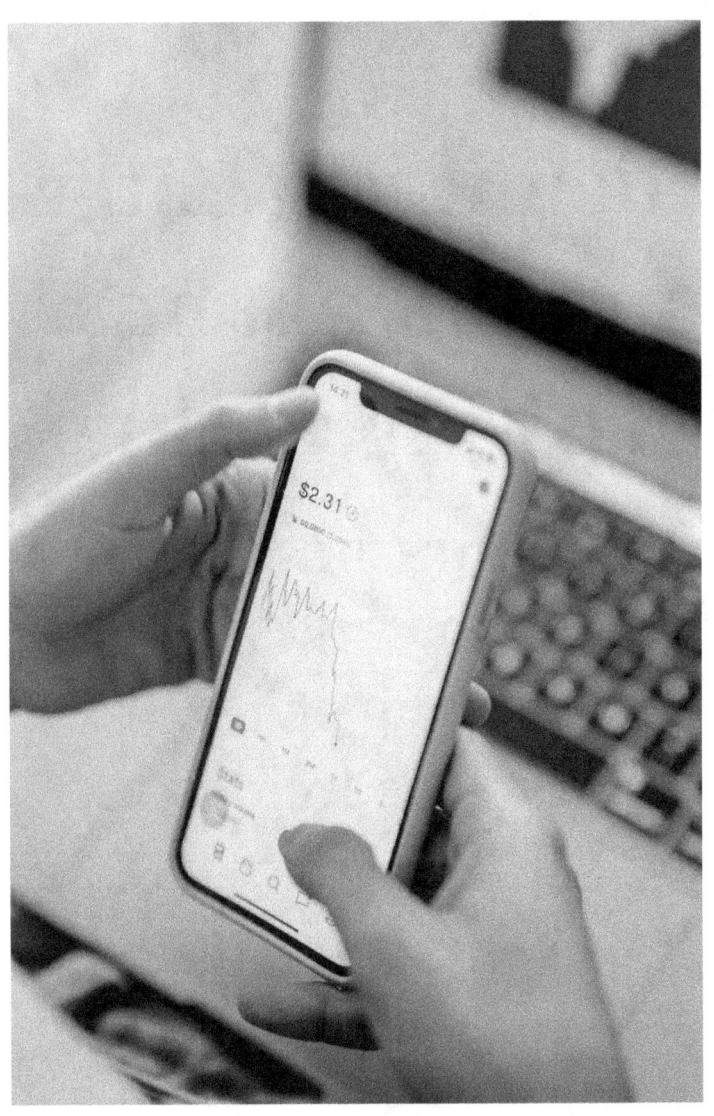

Identifying entry and exit options of Swing trading

Identifying the right entry and exit points is critical to successful swing trading. The following are some key factors to consider when identifying entry and exit options:

1. **Trend analysis:** Traders should identify the current trend of the market and look for opportunities to enter a trade in the direction of the trend. For example, if the market is in an uptrend, traders may look to buy stocks that are likely to rise in value.

2. **Support and resistance levels:**

Support levels are price levels at which buyers tend to step in and purchase an asset, while resistance levels are price levels at which sellers tend to step in and sell an asset. Traders should look for opportunities to enter a trade at support levels and exit at resistance levels.

3. **Technical indicators:** Traders often use technical indicators, such as moving averages, oscillators, and momentum indicators, to help identify entry and exit points. For example, a trader may look for a stock to cross above its moving average to enter a trade, and cross below its

moving average to exit a trade.

4. **Volume analysis:** Traders should also consider the volume of an asset when entering and exiting a trade. High trading volume can indicate a significant level of interest in an asset and may be a sign that the market is about to make a significant move.

5. **Risk management:** It is important to have a well-defined risk management strategy in place when swing trading. This may include setting stop-loss orders to limit potential losses, or using option strategies to manage risk.

It is important to note that no single approach to identifying entry and exit points is guaranteed to be successful, and that traders should consider a combination of factors when making trading decisions. Additionally, market conditions are constantly changing, and traders must continuously monitor their trades and adjust their strategies as needed to stay ahead of the market.

Key technical indicators of Swing trading

Technical indicators are mathematical calculations based on the price and/or volume of an asset that are used to forecast future price movements. The following are some of the key technical indicators that are commonly used in swing trading:

1.   **Moving Averages:** Moving averages are a trend-following indicator that help traders identify the direction of the trend. Simple moving averages (SMA) and exponential moving averages (EMA) are the two most common types of moving averages.

2.   **Bollinger Bands:** Bollinger Bands are volatility indicators that are plotted two standard deviations away from a moving average. They help traders identify overbought and oversold conditions and can be used to generate buy and sell signals.

3.   **Relative Strength Index (RSI):** The RSI

is an oscillator that measures the strength of a stock's price action. It ranges from 0 to 100, and traders look for overbought or oversold conditions by monitoring whether the RSI is above 70 or below 30.

4.   **MACD:** The MACD (Moving Average Convergence Divergence) is a momentum indicator

that measures the relationship between two moving averages. It is often used to generate buy and sell signals, as well as to identify trend changes.

5.   **Stochastic Oscillator:** The stochastic oscillator is an indicator that measures the relationship between a stock's closing price

and its price range over a specific period of time. It is used to identify overbought and oversold conditions and to generate buy and sell signals.

6. **Fibonacci retracements**: Fibonacci retracements are used to identify potential levels of support and resistance in the

market. They are based on the idea that markets will retrace a predictable portion of a move, after which they will continue to move in the original direction.

These are just a few of the many technical indicators that are available to traders. It is important to note that no single indicator is guaranteed to be successful, and that traders should use a combination of indicators in order to make informed trading decisions. Additionally, traders must constantly monitor market conditions and adjust their strategies as needed to stay ahead of the market.

Understanding support and resistance level

Support and resistance levels refer to price points in a financial market where the price tends to experience difficulty in moving past.

Support level is a price point where there is expected to be a demand for the asset, causing the price to stop declining and potentially start rising again.

Resistance level is a price point where there is expected to be an excess supply of the asset, causing the price to stop rising and potentially start declining again.

These levels are widely used in technical analysis for making trading decisions, as well as in setting stop loss and take profit orders.

Reading candlestick charts

A candlestick chart is a type of financial chart used to represent the price movements of an asset, such as a stock or currency, over a specified period of time. Each "candlestick" typically shows one day's worth of price data and consists of four parts:

1.   **The body:** The rectangular part of the candlestick, which represents the difference between the opening and closing price of the asset. If the closing price is higher than the opening price, the body is usually drawn

white or green and is referred to as a "bullish" candle. If the opening price is higher, the body is usually drawn black or red and is referred to as a "bearish" candle.

2.   **The wick:** The thin lines extending from the top and bottom of the body, representing the

highest and lowest prices of the asset during the specified period.

3. **The shadow:** The combination of the upper and lower wick, representing the range of prices the asset traded at during the specified period.

4. **The tail:** The thin line that sometimes appears at the top or bottom of the shadow,

representing a slight extension of the wick beyond the body.

Candlestick charts are useful for visualizing market sentiment and for identifying trends and potential reversal patterns, such as "shooting stars" or "hammer" patterns, which traders may use for making buy or sell decisions.

Setting Stop Losses

A stop loss is an order that is placed to automatically sell a security when it reaches a specified price, designed to limit potential losses in a trade. In swing trading, stop losses are used to manage risk and protect profits.

Here are some tips for setting stop losses in swing trading:

1. **Determine your risk tolerance:** Determine the maximum amount of money you are willing to lose on any

one trade. This will help you to determine the appropriate stop loss level for each trade.

2.   **Use technical analysis:** Analyse the chart of the security you're trading to determine potential levels of support and resistance. You can set your stop loss just below a support level or just above a

resistance level to limit your potential losses.

3. **Consider volatility:** Take into account the volatility of the security you're trading when setting stop losses. If the security is known for large price swings, you may need to set a wider stop loss to allow for normal price movements.

4.   **Trail your stop loss:** Consider adjusting your stop loss as the security's price moves in your favour. You can trail your stop loss by a certain percentage or dollar amount, so that as the security's price rises, your stop loss is also adjusted higher.

It's important to remember that stop losses are not guaranteed and can be executed at a different price than what was specified due to market conditions. However, they can be a useful tool for managing risk in swing trading.

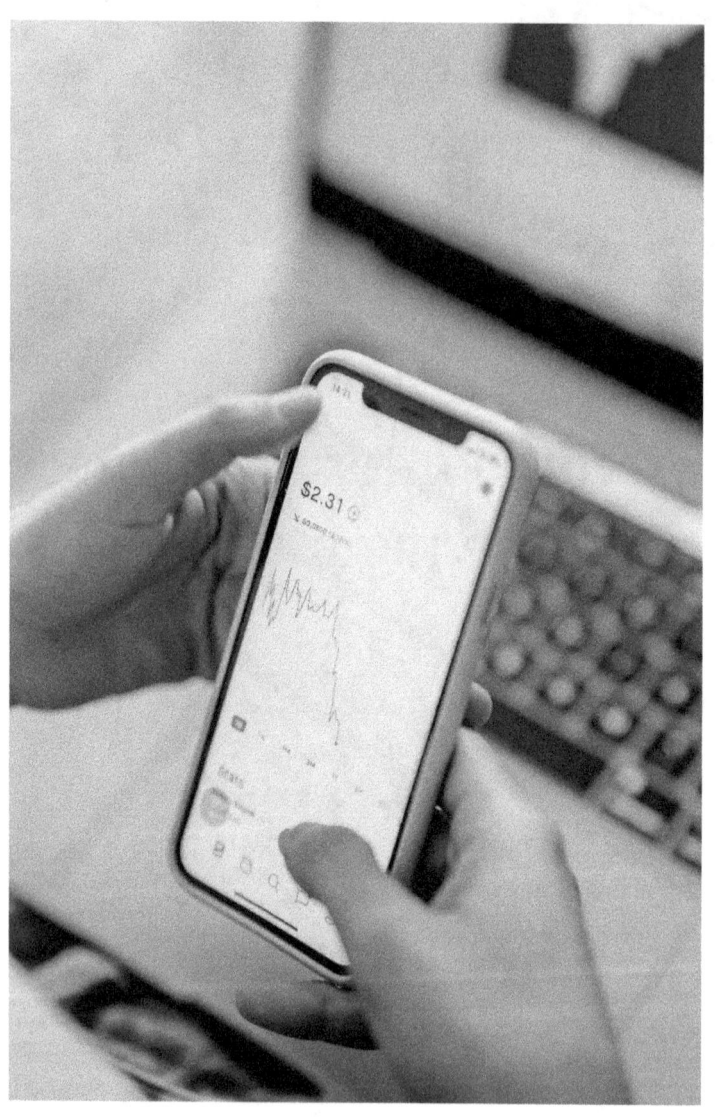

Building a swing trading plan

Building a swing trading plan is an important step in the process of becoming a successful swing trader. Here are the key steps in building a swing trading plan:

1. **Define your goals and risk tolerance:** What are your financial goals and how much risk are

you willing to take to achieve them? These questions should be answered before you start trading.

2. **Choose your markets:** Decide which markets you want to trade, such as stocks, futures, forex, or options. Consider factors such as liquidity, volatility, and cost when making this decision.

3. **Develop your strategy**: Decide on the type of swing trading strategy that best suits your goals and risk tolerance. Some common strategies include trend following, momentum trading, and mean reversion.

4. **Identify entry and exit points:** Use technical indicators and other analysis

tools to identify entry and exit points for your trades. Consider factors such as trend, support and resistance levels, volume, and volatility when making these decisions.

5. **Implement a risk management plan:** Decide on a risk management plan that protects your capital. This may include

setting stop-loss orders, using options strategies, or diversifying your portfolio.

6. **Monitor and adjust your plan:** Monitor your trades and market conditions, and adjust your plan as needed. Keep a record of your trades and analyse your performance to

identify areas where you can improve.

It is important to have a well-defined swing trading plan in place before you start trading. This will help you stay focused, disciplined, and on track as you work towards your trading goals. Additionally, it is important to continuously monitor and adjust your plan as market conditions change in order to stay ahead of the market.

Risk management

Risk management is a critical component of swing trading, as well as any other type of trading. Here are some key elements of a sound risk management plan:

1. **Define your risk tolerance:** Determine the level of risk that you are comfortable taking, based on your

financial goals and personal circumstances.

2.   **Set stop-loss orders:** Stop-loss orders are used to limit potential losses in a trade. They are typically set at a predetermined price level, and will automatically close a trade if the price falls to that level.

3. **Diversify your portfolio:** Diversification helps to reduce the risk of large losses by spreading your investments across multiple markets and asset classes.

4. **Monitor your trades:** Regularly monitor your trades and market conditions, and adjust your positions as

needed to stay ahead of the market.

5.   **Manage your emotions:** Emotional trading decisions can be dangerous, and can lead to impulsive trades that go against your risk management plan. It is important to remain disciplined and stick to your plan, even in the face of market volatility.

6.   **Keep a record of your trades**: Keeping a record of your trades, including entry and exit points, can help you analyse your performance and identify areas where you can improve.

It is important to have a well-defined risk management plan in place before you start trading. This will help you stay disciplined and focused, and will give you the confidence to take advantage of market opportunities without exposing yourself to unnecessary risk. Additionally, it is important to continuously monitor and adjust your risk management plan as market conditions change.

Position sizing

Position sizing is the process of determining the size of your trades based on your risk tolerance and overall trading plan. The goal of position sizing is to maximize returns while minimizing risk. Here are some key factors to consider when determining your position size:

1. **Risk tolerance:** Your position size should be based on the level of risk that you are comfortable taking. Generally, the larger the position size, the higher the risk.

2. **Account size:** Your position size should also be based on the size of your trading account. For example, a larger

trading account may allow for larger position sizes.

3.   **Stop-loss orders:** Stop-loss orders should be set to limit potential losses in a trade. The distance between the entry price and the stop-loss order should be used to determine the maximum size of the trade.

4.   **Volatility:** Volatility, or the degree of price fluctuation, should also be considered when determining your position size. Higher volatility may warrant smaller position sizes.

5.   **Market conditions:** The overall market conditions, such as trend, support and

resistance levels, and volume, should also be considered when determining your position size.

It is important to determine your position size before entering a trade, and to stick to that size throughout the life of the trade. This will help you stay disciplined and focused, and will ensure that your risk is consistent with your overall trading plan. Additionally, it is important to continuously monitor your position size and adjust it as market conditions change.

Setting goals and objective

Setting goals and objectives is an important part of any successful trading strategy, including swing trading. Here are some steps to help you set effective goals and objectives for your swing trading:

1. **Define your financial goals:** Determine the amount

of money that you hope to make from trading, and set specific, achievable goals based on that amount.

2.   **Determine your risk tolerance:** Consider the level of risk that you are comfortable taking, and set goals and objectives that are consistent with that risk tolerance.

3. **Set short-term and long-term goals:** Set both short-term and long-term goals, and prioritize them in order of importance. This will help you stay focused and motivated, and will ensure that you are making progress towards your overall financial goals.

4. **Track your progress:** Regularly

track your progress towards your goals, and adjust your strategy as needed. This will help you stay on track and make necessary changes as market conditions change.

5. **Stay flexible:** Be open to new opportunities and willing to adjust your goals and objectives as necessary. This

will help you stay adaptable and responsive to changes in market conditions.

Having clear and well-defined goals and objectives will help you stay focused and motivated, and will give you a roadmap to follow as you pursue your trading strategy. Additionally, regularly reviewing and adjusting your goals and objectives will help ensure that they remain relevant and achievable, and that you are making progress towards your overall financial goals.

Developing a trading plan

Developing a trading plan is a crucial step in the process of swing trading, as it helps to define your strategy, set clear goals, and manage risk. Here are some key elements of a successful swing trading plan:

1. **Define your strategy:** Determine the specific market

conditions and technical indicators that you will use to identify swing trade opportunities.

2. **Set goals and objectives:** Determine your financial goals, risk tolerance, and the level of capital that you are willing to allocate to swing trading.

3. **Identify entry and exit points:** Use technical analysis and market research to identify the key levels at which you will enter and exit trades.

4. **Determine position size**: Use position sizing techniques to determine the size of your trades based on your risk tolerance

and overall trading plan.

5.   **Plan for risk management:** Develop a risk management plan to help limit potential losses and protect your capital.

6.   **Monitor and review:** Regularly monitor your trades, market conditions, and overall performance, and

adjust your plan as
needed.

Having a well-defined
trading plan will help you
stay disciplined and
focused, and will ensure
that you are following a
consistent and systematic
approach to swing
trading. Additionally,
regularly reviewing and
updating your plan will
help ensure that it
remains relevant and
effective, and that you

are making progress
towards your overall
financial goals.

Implementing swing trading plan

Implementing your swing trading plan involves putting the steps outlined in your plan into action. Here are some key steps to help you implement your swing trading plan effectively:

1. **Start small:** Begin by trading small positions and gradually increasing your size as you gain experience and confidence.

2. **Stay disciplined:** Stick to your trading plan and avoid deviating from it, especially during

times of market volatility.

3. **Keep a trading journal:** Document your trades, including the reasons for entering and exiting them, to help you track your progress and improve your performance over time.

4. **Use stop-loss orders:** Use stop-loss orders to limit

potential losses and protect your capital.

5. **Monitor the market**: Regularly monitor the market, including economic data releases, news events, and technical indicators, to stay up-to-date on market conditions.

6. **Stay patient:** Swing trading can be a slow and steady process, and it is

important to be
patient and wait for
the right opportunities
to present themselves.
7. **Manage risk:**
Continuously monitor
and manage risk, and
adjust your position
size as market
conditions change.

By following these steps
and staying disciplined,
you can increase the
chances of success in
your swing trading

endeavours. It is important to remember that trading is a journey, and that consistency and persistence over time is key to achieving your goals.

Finding stocks to trade

Finding stocks to trade is an important step in the swing trading process. Here are some steps to help you find suitable stocks for swing trading:

1.   **Start with a watchlist:** Identify a list of stocks that you are interested in trading and monitor

their movements over time.

2. **Look for stocks with high liquidity:** Focus on stocks that have high trading volume, as this will help ensure that you can enter and exit trades with ease.

3. **Consider the fundamentals:** Look for stocks with strong financials, including positive earnings and

revenue growth, to increase your chances of success.

4.   **Use technical analysis:** Use technical analysis tools, such as trend lines, moving averages, and chart patterns, to identify potential trade opportunities.

5.   **Monitor market trends:** Stay up-to-date on market trends

and sector-specific news, as this can help you identify potential opportunities.

6. **Consider sector and market trends**: Consider the overall market trends, as well as trends within specific sectors, to help identify potential opportunities.

7. **Seek out opportunities in volatile markets:**

Volatile markets can provide swing trading opportunities, so consider stocks that are showing significant price swings.

By following these steps and using a combination of fundamental and technical analysis, you can increase your chances of finding suitable stocks for swing trading. Additionally, it is

important to remember to
continually monitor and
reassess your positions,
and to adjust your
strategy as market
conditions change.

Executing trades

Executing trades is an important step in the swing trading process, as it requires quick and effective decision-making. Here are some key steps to help you execute trades successfully:

1. **Identify entry points:** Use your trading plan and technical analysis to

identify potential entry points for your trades.

2.   **Place orders:** Use your broker's platform to place your orders, including entry and exit orders and stop-loss orders.

3.   **Monitor your positions:** Regularly monitor your positions and stay up-to-date on market conditions, including

economic data releases and news events.

4. **Adjust orders as needed**: Make any necessary adjustments to your orders, including adjusting stop-loss orders and adjusting position size, as market conditions change.

5. **Exit positions:** Use your technical analysis and market

research to determine when it is time to exit your positions, and execute your exit orders promptly.

By following these steps, you can increase the chances of success in your swing trading endeavours. It is important to remember that trading requires discipline and patience, and that quick and emotional decision-making can lead to poor outcomes. Additionally, it is important to continuously monitor and reassess your trades, and to adjust your strategy as market conditions change.

Monitoring your trades

Monitoring your trades is a crucial step in the swing trading process, as it helps you stay on top of market conditions and make informed decisions. Here are some key steps to help you effectively monitor your trades:

1. **Keep a trading journal:** Document your trades, including

the reasons for entering and exiting them, to help you track your progress and improve your performance over time.

2.   **Monitor market conditions:** Stay up-to-date on market conditions, including economic data releases, news events, and technical indicators, to stay

informed about market trends.

3.   **Check your positions regularly:** Regularly check your positions and assess their performance, and make any necessary adjustments as market conditions change.

4.   **Use stop-loss orders:** Use stop-loss orders to limit potential losses and

protect your capital, and adjust these orders as market conditions change.

5.   **Reassess your strategy:** Regularly reassess your trading plan and strategy, and make any necessary adjustments as you gain experience and improve your performance.

By following these steps and staying disciplined,

you can increase the chances of success in your swing trading endeavours. Additionally, it is important to remember to be patient and not to make impulsive decisions based on short-term market fluctuations. Continuously monitoring your trades and adjusting your strategy as needed can help you achieve your long-term trading goals.

Making adjustment to your plan

Making adjustments in your swing trading plan is an important part of the trading process, as market conditions and individual circumstances can change over time. Here are some key steps to help you make effective adjustments in your swing trading plan:

1. **Reassess your strategy:** Regularly reassess your swing trading plan and strategy, taking into account any changes in market conditions and your personal circumstances.

2. **Adjust position sizing**: Consider adjusting your position sizing, either increasing or decreasing it based on

market conditions and your personal risk tolerance.

3.   **Modify your entry and exit criteria:** As you gain experience, consider modifying your entry and exit criteria to improve your performance and increase the chances of success.

4.   **Consider new technical indicators:**

Consider incorporating new technical indicators into your analysis, as this can help you identify potential trade opportunities.

5. **Stay up-to-date on market trends:** Stay informed about market trends, including sector-specific news, economic data releases, and technical

analysis, to make informed decisions.

By following these steps and continually adjusting your plan as needed, you can increase your chances of success in your swing trading endeavours. Additionally, it is important to remember to be disciplined and patient, and to avoid making impulsive decisions based on short-term market fluctuations. Continuously monitoring your trades and adjusting your plan as needed can help you achieve your long-term trading goals.

Advanced swing trading techniques

Advanced swing trading options refer to more complex strategies and techniques that experienced traders may use to improve their performance and increase the chances of success. Here are some of the advanced options in swing trading:

1.   **Options trading:**
Incorporating options
into your swing
trading strategy can
help you to hedge
your positions,
increase your returns,
and reduce your risk.
2.   **Short selling**:
Short selling involves
selling a stock you do
not own with the hope
of buying it back at a
lower price, allowing

you to profit from a declining market.

3. **Multileg trading:** Multileg trading involves placing multiple orders at the same time, often with the goal of benefiting from market volatility.

4. **Algorithmic trading**: Algorithmic trading uses computer algorithms to make trades based on pre-

determined rules and conditions, allowing for faster and more precise trade execution.

5.   **Trend following:** Trend following involves using technical analysis to identify market trends and make trades accordingly, often with the goal of benefiting from long-

term market movements.

While these advanced options can help traders to achieve their goals, it is important to be aware of the added risks and complexities that can come with these strategies. As such, it is important for traders to thoroughly research and understand these advanced options before incorporating them into their swing trading strategy. Additionally, it is always a good idea to seek professional advice from a financial advisor or a licensed trader before making any investment decisions.

Swing trading with options

Swing trading with options is a strategy where a trader combines stock and option trades to take advantage of market trends and volatility. The objective of this strategy is to generate returns from short-term price movements in a stock, while also using options to manage risk. Here are some key steps to swing trading with options:

1. **Identify the underlying stock:** Choose a stock that you believe is poised for a price move and has options available for trading.

2. **Choose the right option:** Decide on the type of option you want to trade, such as a call option or a put option, based on your

market outlook and risk tolerance.

3.   **Set entry and exit criteria:** Determine your entry and exit criteria for both your stock and option trades, including how you will manage risk.

4.   **Execute the trade**: Once you have identified the stock and option that meet your criteria, execute your trade, buying the

stock and selling the option at the same time.

5.   **Monitor your trades:** Regularly monitor your trades, especially in the case of options where the value of the option may change quickly.

While swing trading with options can be a profitable strategy, it is important to understand the risks involved, including the risk of the stock price declining and the option expiring worthless. Additionally, it is important to thoroughly research and understand the mechanics of options trading before incorporating them into your swing trading strategy. It is also recommended to seek professional advice from a financial advisor or a licensed options trader

before making any
investment decisions.

Swing trading with futures

Swing trading with futures refers to a trading strategy in which traders hold futures contracts for intermediate periods of time, usually a few days to several weeks, with the aim of profiting from price swings or market volatility. Swing traders in futures markets often use technical analysis and/or fundamental analysis to identify potential trade opportunities and manage risk. It is important to note that futures trading can be a highly leveraged and volatile market, so it's crucial for swing traders to have a solid understanding of market dynamics, risk management techniques, and the use of stop-loss orders.

Swing trading with Forex

Swing trading with forex refers to a trading strategy in which traders hold foreign currency positions for intermediate periods of time, usually a few days to several weeks, with the aim of profiting from price swings or market volatility. Swing traders in the forex market often use technical analysis and/or fundamental analysis to identify potential trade opportunities and manage risk. It is important to note that forex trading can be highly leveraged and volatile, so it's crucial for swing traders to have a solid understanding of market dynamics, risk management techniques, and the use of stop-loss orders. Additionally, it's important for forex traders to understand the impact of global economic and political events on currency exchange rates.

Final thought on swing trading

Swing trading can be a profitable approach for

traders who have a solid understanding of market dynamics, technical and/or fundamental analysis, and risk management. However, it is important to keep in mind that like any other form of trading, swing trading also involves significant risk, especially given the use of leverage in many markets. Therefore, it's crucial for swing traders to have a well-defined trading plan and to be disciplined in executing that plan, including the use of stop-loss orders to manage risk. Before engaging in swing trading, it is recommended to gain a comprehensive understanding of the market and to seek the advice of a financial professional.

Thanking you....
The end....